Real Estate Note Investing

*How Buying Distressed and Profitable Mortgages
Can Skyrocket Your Income*

Vincent Norris

Contents

Introduction

Congratulations on downloading *Retail Estate Note Investing: How Buying Distressed and Profitable Mortgages Can Skyrocket Your Investment Income* and thank you for doing so.

The following chapters will illustrate the various ways you can make money by purchasing real estate loans and turn a high profit with a fraction of the work you would do for a hard real estate. This market is "investor-only" territory; be prepared to play in the major leagues to make the major money. Thankfully, what may appear scary and daunting in the beginning will seem like a minimal risk by the end of this book. You may even begin strategizing on how to invest in commercial real estate notes by the time you finish this book!

As with any investment, there come questions and concerns. This book covers a range of those as well, along with tips and ideas on how to minimize the risk. Things like changes in the market, environmental problems, or borrower challenges can hinder your success. But read on to learn how to approach these scenarios along with suggestions on how to develop relationships that reap you the high rewards. Example phrases and conversations are included, too, so you feel confident in setting the right tone right away. In addition to giving you tips on how to handle several of the nuances of investing in real estate notes, you will learn tips on how to find the best opportunities for the best price. After all, the lower you buy a good note, the better return you can get! So, now get ready to learn all about real estate note investing and skyrocket your investment income through the roof!

There are plenty of books on this subject on the market, thanks again for choosing this one! Every effort was made to ensure it is full of as much useful information as possible, please enjoy!

Chapter 1: Introduction to How Mortgage Notes Work

So you are considering investing in real estate notes, but first, you need to learn what exactly these notes are and how they work. This chapter's goal is to outline the various forms of mortgage notes you can choose and how each can be purchased and become profitable. The focus is on residential real estate mortgage notes. Commercial mortgage notes will be discussed further on in this book.

To begin, let us investigate the central conditions considered for the different kinds of mortgage notes: performing/sub-performing/non-performing notes, liens, location, and collateral. While reviewing the descriptions of each criterion below, determine what combination will work best for your own situation. Consider your finances, objectives, and time commitment. This includes how you tolerate problems, numbers, and stress. While it is a good idea to identify your strategy as you review, keep in mind you can always diversify your investments as you review and pursue a deal.

Performing/Sub-performing/Non-performing Notes

There are three types of notes you will encounter: performing, sub-performing, and non-performing. A performing note refers to a loan that is being paid on time by the borrower. You can check if a loan is performing by checking with the lender. A sale price for a performing note ranges between 75% and 100% of the present value of the note. A sub-performing note refers to a loan that has a late payment anywhere from fifteen days to two months late. The lender can contact the borrower to become current but can still be sold when it is "newly" late. A sale price for a sub-performing note ranges from 50% to 80% of the present value of the note. A non-performing note is the most common type of note investing. This refers to a loan that is in default and repayment is not expected in terms of the original agreement. A sale price for a non-performing note ranges between 10% and 50% of the present value of the note. This is why it is the most attractive investment option.

A non-performing loan requires a decent amount of work to resolve the problem. You need to determine if you are willing to put in the work to turn this type of loan around. Balance your time against your finances. If you find that you have more time than money, choosing a non-performing loan can be a good strategy. On the other hand, if money is more ready at that time, it is a wise idea to begin note investing by choosing performing notes instead. This is because a loan with a positive cash flow after is because non-performing means you can generate a return of around 15% and does not require a lot of extra work to generate that income. Many times an investor will sell their loans that are performing to re-exploit and purchase additional loans that are non-performing. There are several performing notes available to purchase almost all the time.

Liens

There are two main types of liens on notes: junior and senior, or second and first position. This is one of the most important considerations when debating buying a mortgage note; it is potentially the least important compared with the other three criteria. This is because there is little difference between the two types of liens. The two can foreclose in the same manner, and reward-from-risk is comparable between junior and senior liens, as long as you are diligent.

Junior Liens

This type of loan provides additional resources for the money. Withholding late fees and interest, the percentage of the chief balance determines the price of a junior lien. Typically, for an average quality asset, this is approximately 30% of the UPB or "unpaid principal balance". Another benefit is the savings of approximately $200 for each asset because you do not need to pay for tax information, BPO's, title reports, and BPO's or broker's price opinion while doing your due diligence.

While reviewing the credit report of the borrower, look for senior loans and review their balance and status. This is the primary element for consideration for investing in a junior, or secondary, lien. You can tell a borrower's intent if the loans are current and they are making payments, even if the value of the loan is more than the value of the property, or there is negative equity. In addition, the majority of companies that handle senior liens escrow insurance and taxes for the borrower. To explain, it is likely that there are no late taxes and insurance on the property if a senior lien is current. Occasionally, it is possible to receive a good reward when a senior lien is late or not known. If you buy a note with the identical sum of investment, it allows you to diversify with additional assets if you choose junior liens over a senior. Your risk can provide an attractive reward.

Senior Liens

These forms of liens are typically a preferred form of debt, which means that they are usually sold for a higher price. The property value, or the collateral's underlying value, is how the seller of the loan determines the basic price. Purchasing a senior lien requires you to do more due diligence and it is more expensive to analyze the lien. This is because you need to determine that the lien is actually sitting in a priority spot by securing a title report. In addition, you must find past-due tax balances by researching online or calling. This is critical prior to purchasing this type of lien, as is observing the condition and value of the property. This is because resolution for senior liens is typically done through the property more so than junior liens. What is more important is a demographic analysis of the zip code and research for comparable properties. Your outlook on the property can be swiftly altered by one poor BPO.

Location

This consideration is strictly aligned with your personal goals and desires. You can decide to pinpoint a precise location or across the country; it all depends on your preference. If you decide to work across the country, you can expect to receive the greatest deals because you can purchase in a mixed and bulk asset. However, it does require you to have a broader understanding of various local markets and create a web of vendors and attorneys around the nation. Generally, it is easier to invest in junior liens across the country than it is for senior liens.

Should you decide to invest in a specific geographic location, you must first determine the market, either locally or more broad, such as your state. Being near the location is an advantage even though you will probably never actually visit the property. Another great advantage to having a precise location is your capability to focus on understanding the unique local processes and cultivate strong relationships with attorneys and other vendors.

If a state is non-judicial or judicial is the most important difference between investments in various states. Keep in mind that it is possible to be both a judicial and non-judicial state. Foreclosures typically take a greater amount of time in judicial states. Foreclosures can be completed within just a couple months in non-judicial states, but it can take over a year in judicial states. New Jersey and New York are known for taking the longest time. This lengthy turn-around time is because the court system determines the foreclosure in judicial states. Below is a list of states, and if they are one or another or both, including an average of how long it takes to foreclose and redeem:

State	J (judicial) NJ (non-judicial) B (both)	Foreclosure Time	Redemption Time
AL	B	1 to 3 Months	Up to 12 Months
AK	B	3 to 4 Months	N/A

AZ	B	3 to 4 Months	Up to 6 Months
AK	B	4 to 5 Months	Up to 12 Months
CA	B	3 to 5 Months	Dubious
CO	B	2 to 5 Months	N/A
CT	J	5 to 6 Months	Determined by Court
DE	J	3 to 7 Months	N/A
D.C.	NJ	2 to 4 Months	N/A
FL	J	4 to 6 Months	YES
GA	B	2 to 3 Months	N/A
HI	B	3 to 4 Months	N/A
ID	B	5 to 6 Months	N/A
IL	J	7 to 10 Months	Up to 7 Months
IN	J	5 to 7 Months	N/A
IA	B	5 to 6 Months	Up to 12 Months
KS	J	3 to 5 Months	Up to 12 Months
KT	J	5 to 6 Months	Up to 12 Months
LA	J	2 to 6 Months	N/A
ME	J	6 to 10 Months	Up to 3 Months
MD	J	2 to 3 Months	Determined by Court
MA	J	3 to 4 Months	N/A
MI	NJ	2 to 3 Months	Up to 12 Months
MN	B	2 to 3 Months	Up to 6 Months
MS	B	2 to 3 Months	N/A
MO	B	2 to 3 Months	Up to 12 Months
MT	B	4 to 6 Months	Up to 12 Months
NE	J	5 to 6 Months	N/A
NV	B	3 to 5 Months	N/A
NH	NJ	2 to 3 Months	N/A
NJ	J	3 to 10 Months	Up to 6 Months

State			
NM	J	4 to 6 Months	Up to 9 Months
NY	J	4 to 8 Months	N/A
NC	B	2 to 4 Months	Up to 10 Days
ND	J	3 to 5 Months	Up to 2 Months
OH	J	5 to 7 Months	When Confirmed
OK	B	4 to 7 Months	When Confirmed
OR	B	4 to 6 Months	N/A
PA	J	3 to 9 Months	N/A
RI	B	2 to 3 Months	Up to 3 YRS
SC	J	4 to 7 Months	N/A
SD	B	6 to 9 Months	Up to 12 Months
TN	NJ	2 to 3 Months	Up to 2 YRS
TX	B	2 to 3 Months	N/A
UT	N/A	4 to 5 Months	Up to 1 ½ YRS
VT	J	7 to 10 Months	Up to 6 Months
VA	B	2 to 3 Months	N/A
WA	B	4 to 5 Months	N/A
WV	NJ	2 to 3 Months	N/A
WI	B	6 to 10 Months	N/A
WY	B	2 to 3 Months	Up to 3 Months

Collateral

In the residential market, there are several various criteria for real estate. The furthermost common includes condo, land, multi-family, manufactured and single family. The property most often financed is a single family, of SFR. A multi-family, or MFR or MDU, includes properties like triplexes and duplexes. Condos are a single unit of a larger building. Manufactured homes are prefabricated buildings such as mobile homes. Land refers to vacant property that is raw or practically undeveloped with no structures built on it.

SFR or MFR properties are best for new note investors because they are less risk and they are of greater quality. When you become more experienced and can take on more risk, consider investing in manufactured or land mortgage notes.

How to Invest In Mortgage Notes

The best way to make money in note investing involves using your skills to the best of your ability. It is true you can outsource almost all of the areas you do not want to or cannot handle; however, the most money lies in a purchase that uses the majority of your skills without major outside delegations. Therefore, you need to decide if you prefer to work in the field or in the office.

The "field" means you enjoy and are good at working with your hands, helping with repairs, turning over tenants, and conducting real estate showings as required. The "office" means searching for new leads, being a negotiator for various deals, and keep the process and paperwork organized. Thankfully, with the availability and mobility of the internet and laptops all over, you can take your "office" wherever you need to be. Remember, much of note investing is not at the property but rather on your phone and computer. This is an important consideration now for you to decide.

Additional considerations are listed below to outline the difference between other real estate investment strategies versus real estate note investments:

Rental Property Investments

There are two investment strategies for rental property: "buy and keep" or "fix and flip." To purchase a rental property and to hold on to it requires you to be a strong negotiator and do a lot of work upfront. You must make high-quality repairs and select the best tenants to rent the asset. This is a long-term strategy, but it has the benefit of passive income. The best way to keep this investment profitable is for you to do the majority of the upkeep and choose quality rental properties. You can find a profit with the property that you hold and contract the work out, however, it is not scalable. The stress of up-keeping a house means you can expect to feel like it is more of a liability than an asset.

Should you decide to take on a property to "fix and flip," you will be focused on turning over the property as soon as possible. There is no opportunity for passive income with this method because you will be moving from one deal to the next. The best method for success is to have a well-organized office setting to keep leads consistent and also in the field, helping and overseeing the work being done.

Mortgage Note Investments

Just like rental properties, you can choose to purchase and keep a performing note or fix up and flip a non-performing note. If you are an investor looking for passive investments, this buying and keeping a note is a wise choice, especially if you do not have a lot of time but plenty of money to put in. This strategy allows you to stay away from the property and you do not need to do a lot of work on the front end. It is very similar to purchasing a rental property to hold on to because it has a tenant, but this one means you do not need to ever do any up-keep on the property yourself. The problem or risk you take is that the tenant will no longer pay you once the loan has been paid off. This means the property is only profitable for about ten years.

Unlike fixing and flipping a house, putting in this type of work on a note requires less time and yields a higher return. There is more time involved in purchasing the note that in a "fix and flip" house and even a performing note. However, turning a non-performing note around after you purchase it does not take as long as it takes to fix up a house. Also, you do not need to be hands-on in the renovations like a "fix and flip" house. Once you turn the note into a performing note, you can now choose to sell it or keep it for passive income.

Chapter 2: Overview of Note Investing Strategies

Choosing to invest in a note is a wonderful strategy for long-term cash flow, especially because if the tenant stops paying you to have the asset you can use for a profit. Instead of collecting rent, now you can sell the property, rent it out, or fix and flip it. The largest difference between being a "landlord" and owning the property as a rental and being the "note holder" and holding the loan the borrower is paying on, means you do not have to keep up the property yourself. You do not need to pay for maintenance, insurance, or taxes. You are now the "bank" for the homeowner. Ideally, you will have a company to service the loan so they can confirm the borrower is paying and on time. These records are important for you to ensure on-time passive income, but also in the future should you decide to unload the note down the road.

When considering your profit potential, keep in mind that having a company service your note costs an average of about $16 per month or around $200 per year. In comparison, a property manager can charge up to 10% of the rent per month and ask for up to 100% of the first month's rent to find a tenant. Another consideration is the difference between paying off a note compared to the appreciation of a rental property over time. This may sound like a negative consequence to purchasing a note versus a rental property. However, ideally, you have purchased a note far below the value of the asset, which means your coupon rate, or the note's interest rate, is higher. It is important to realize that the interest rate you receive is on the contract price, regardless of how much you have paid for it. In addition, you are receiving principal payments which often offer a larger return.

There are a few different reasons to purchase a note. You were introduced to a little bit in the previous chapter, however, here you will explore more investment strategies to determine what is the best plan for your goals. Some of the different investment strategies include property acquisition, wholesale, and flipping. Also, you will have the opportunity to explore the different options between junior and senior loan strategies.

<u>*Note Investment for Property Acquisition*</u>

Foreclosures are a hard reality that many have faced, especially since the devastating crash in 2008/2009. Maybe you had the unfortunate experience of going through a foreclosure or know someone who has. In the least, you have probably seen the vacant houses falling into disrepair in the neighborhoods. Buying the note from a lender is an excellent method for getting a property at a low price. Because the bank has not foreclosed on the property yet, they are willing to offload the note at a significantly lowered price compared to a real estate owned property. Also, there is an uncertainty with a non-performing note resulting in less competition to get it. Once you get ahold of the note, you need to vacate the tenant, fix the property as needed, and sell it at the valued price. Many investors who specialize in flipping do not go after non-performing liens to acquire property, and it is a risk for flipper's because the owner can make payments and they are no longer able to foreclose the property. Another complication is if the property owner declares bankruptcy.

<u>*Note Investment- Wholesaling*</u>

Just like wholesaling a property, you can wholesale a note. The challenge is that you do not own the property or asset, just the loan, and it is under contract. There is a term called a "daisy chain" in note wholesaling that refers to a string of wholesaler's selling off a note that is under contract. If you get caught at the end, there can be a lengthy process involved in untangling the paperwork and collateral for the asset. It is a racket that you should try to avoid. Wholesaling requires you work with reputable and reliable people, so find people you can trust to buy and trade with. The basics of this methods require you to find sellers who are motivated, purchase the asset at a low cost from the seller, and offload the note for more than you paid as soon as possible.

Note Investment- Flipping

Just like flipping a house, you can flip a note. The difference is that you are not remodeling a bathroom or painting a wall. You are getting your borrower to make on-time payments again for a period of time so you can sell it at a higher price as a performing note. Or you can keep the note for a source of passive income now that it is performing. The benefit is the large return you can expect once the note turns from non-performing to re-performing. There are a variety of ways you can get a note re-performing again. For example, you can nudge the borrower to refinance in an effort to secure a lower interest rate, offer a credit-repair plan, or give them an incentive with a discount on the principal payment for refinancing within a predetermined time frame. Strategies like this are most advantageous for borrowers that are facing high-interest rates, so search for non-performing notes with higher interest rates. Just remember, the borrower already got into a situation with a previous lender despite knowing what they could do to get out of a bad situation. It is possible that they will not follow through on the strategy, despite knowing the benefits. For this reason, always have a backup plan.

Junior Lien Investment Strategies

Investing in a non-performing junior lien is attractive because of the deep discount on the purchase price. Often you will find these types of loans completely or partially underwater. The main strategy is to get the lien re-performing again because foreclosure would still leave the senior lien in existence. To minimize risk, find a non-performing junior lien that has a performing senior lien and determine the borrower's quality for payment instead of on the value of the property and collateral. Also, check for government liens on the property. The government has the highest priority on a note and can take control of the property if they need to, regardless of the note you hold. This would wipe your note out and leave you with no profit potential.

No Equity on Non-performing Junior Liens

It is worth considering the second lien even if it does not have equity. This type of lien should be purchased at a very low cost, and it should have a history of on-time and consistent payments with a borrower that is invested in the property. The ideal situation is a much steeper discount on the UPB in hopes of a larger return.

No Equity on Performing Senior Lien with Non-performing Junior Lien

This is one of the largest risks you can take on note investing but can offer some of the highest returns if your work is right and invest wisely. At the right price, investing in a junior lien that shows a history of on-time payments to the senior lien, but the junior lien has become delinquent from a temporary situation, means they will probably be able to bring the junior lien re-performing again with little intervention in the meantime. You could offer to modify the loan to spread payments over a longer span of time or reduce the principal to get them current again. Notes that fall into this category are often referred to as "junk" notes so you can get them for a great price and have little competition for them.

Investments like this require the borrower to be emotionally invested in their property; understanding how long they have lived in the house, if it was passed down through the family, if they work nearby, their children attend school in the district, and their involvement in the community are all good indicators that they are invested emotionally in staying in their property. Also, if the property appears to be well cared for or maintained is another indicator of an invested borrower. Despite emotional investment, it is critical that the borrower shows the ability to become current on the note. If they do not have a way to keep their property, do not invest in the "junk" note.

Senior Lien Investment Strategies

Just like junior lien strategies as described in the first chapter, there is a difference between performing and non-performing notes for senior liens. The difference in strategy between junior and senior is that a senior lien is considered the higher priority lien, so you can foreclose without being left "holding the bag" like you would be with a junior lien.

Non-performing Senior Liens

Banks have a plethora of these on their books and would rather offload the note than go through the hassle of foreclosing. This is why you can get them for pennies on the dollar. To get out of the note, there are a few different strategies to consider:

1. Foreclose- This is the only choice for the note sometimes. Unfortunately, it takes a lot of time and there are additional legal and holding costs to consider. The good thing about this option is that it clears the junior liens and creates a clean title.
2. Short sale- Because you are now the "bank," you can allow the borrower to do a short sale on the property to pay off the note. Unfortunately, junior liens can make this option a challenge because they need to be cleared prior to the sale.
3. Deed-in-lieu- When the borrower cannot bring their note current, you can take over the property from the borrower. They would sign over the property to you to satisfy the debt. If there is a junior lien on the property, it will remain for you to address or pay off, so keep that in mind with this exit strategy.
4. Workout- Making modifications to help a borrower become current on their note saves them from a foreclosure and helps you gather interest and principal on your investment. It can provide a long-term, passive income for you or you can sell it at a higher price now that it is performing. People

stop paying for a variety of reasons. Finding out if it is because they got underwater and did not see a point in paying, or they lost their job and got behind with no end in sight. When you find out what has happened, you can offer a variety of options to help them stay in their home and not suffer a foreclosure on their record. This is the most advantageous exit strategy for everyone involved.

Performing Senior Liens- Buy and Hold

As described in chapter one, you can purchase a lien and hold on to it for passive income until the loan is paid off. This can last ten years or longer. The difference between owning a rental property and a note is that you are not responsible for the property upkeep and fees. The return is usually lower on these notes, but it is typically steady and reliable - less risk. A seller wants to cash out of a real estate investment typically, instead of getting payments each month, so they are willing to sell at a slightly discounted price from the value of the property.

Performing Senior Liens- "Buy long - sell short"

"Money today is worth more than money tomorrow." – M. Cofield

Value degrades over time. This approach takes advantage of this and the strategy is known as "partial." This tactic allows you to buy a loan that is performing at a discounted price and sell a few of the higher-valued payments from the beginning of the lien while saving the lower, back-end payments. By selling the beginning of the lien, you can potentially make an additional profit by selling the front end of the loan while reaping the benefits of the low-end payments at the end of the loan. Because the note is still in your name, you retain the asset but can recoup the original investment sooner rather than later.

Chapter 3: Overview of Non-performing Lien Investing

Below is a step-by-step guide on how to approach a non-performing note:

1. Establish relationships with note lenders, such as credit unions, banks, and hedge funds.
2. Review and understand the details on the loan information spreadsheet, or "tape," for the property.
3. Prepare to negotiate with the original lender based on the information on the "tape."
4. Enter your "indicative bid," purchase offer, or LOI, which stands for "letter of intent".
5. Review the loan documents and paperwork related to the collateral when you receive it to make sure everything is in order.
6. Close and take over the note when you finalize the purchase.
7. Begin working with the borrower to "workout" the loan or begin implementing your exit strategy for the note.
8. Once the exit strategy is complete, which can range from days to years, you will need to resettle your rights for the asset.
9. How to transfer your rights in a sale.

The process can appear lengthy, but really the profit potential is large after you learn what to do.

Purchasing a note that is not performing can range from wildly profitable to a slim margin. Of course, buying a performing lien is still a risk. However, choosing a non-performing note without research and understanding can tie you up in a negative investment for years. There are steps you need to take to improve your odds of a positive return and even create a large one. One of the most important considerations is collateral. The other is understanding the borrower. Especially if you are considering a second lien, the borrower plays a key role. When you evaluate a borrower, as alluded to earlier, you need to consider the equity established by the emotional connection of the borrower to the property. If they are willing to assist you and are also able to help in the process, you could find yourself in the ideal "win/win" scenario.

One way to tell if a borrower is connected to their property is to look at the condition of the house. A borrower that is proud of their house is evident in the upkeep they attempt to the asset. Are there plants maintained around the house? Is the lawn mowed and cared for? Comparing a borrower's credit history with their "emotional equity" is an art and can illustrate the full picture.

Side Note: Working with the Borrower

The challenge with non-performing liens is that the borrower has already shown that they are willing to not follow through on their commitment to their loan. They did not work out arrangements with their previous lender, either because they could not or did not know it was an option, and therefore got behind in payments. When you step into your new note, you need to get in contact with them right away and show them that you mean business. Letting them know that you are looking for the "win/win" for both of you, and that you are determined and serious about it, you can begin the workout process.

An example of how you can show this to your borrower is by saying:

"You are going to have a great day today. A bank no longer owns your loan, a person does. Together we can work to resolve your troubles and achieve progressive results, which a bank cannot accomplish."

By creating this relationship, you show to your borrower that you do not view them as a number, that you value them as a person, you want them to be successful, and you have compassion. This relationship is your best guarantee of getting your payments on time for the length of the agreement.

Another example of how to establish a serious note to your relationship is to play the "good cop" side to an anonymous "bad cop." Saying something along the lines of:

"If you ever have a problem, always contact me immediately and directly. I am here to help you and we can find a solution together. (This is you being the "good cop"). *Your payments go directly to my attorney, and if they are ever late, he does not wait to start the foreclosure proceedings. That will end up costing you thousands and can make buying a home in the future more challenging.* (This is the anonymous "bad cop"). *I want to avoid that happening at all costs for you."*

This means that if your borrower ever called you to explain that they have lost their job or need to take time off work for medical reasons, you can decide what a reasonable monthly payment would be to keep them in the habit of paying each month without having them get behind again. Maybe instead of paying the agreed-upon $500 each month, you find out that they can commit to $100 per month for a period of two months, and then it will go back to the original payment once they are back at work. You can record them as current on their payments and tack on the balance that they did not pay during that time to the loan's backend. This flexibility is unique agreement that a bank will almost never do. By working with your borrower, you can keep the note performing and now you have a grateful and loyal borrower living in your asset.

Finding a Non-performing Lien

Before you can get to the point of talking with a borrower, you first need to find a lien. There are a few different places you can look. Where you decide to buy from will depend on the amount of money you can and will invest into the note, and the amount of work that you want to put into it. Below are a couple of places you can look for a non-performing note:

1. *Purchase from a hedge fund*: This is probably the easiest method for buying a non-performing lien. These private groups are large and purchase several non-performing liens to wholesale for a good return. Typically, when they buy in bulk they get a better deal. When they get these notes, they can exit the note how they see fit, including selling off some to other investors. The problem with this method is that you are getting the "seconds" or "hand-me-down's". By the time the asset gets to you as the final buyer, it has been passed over several times for one reason or another and it has been found unworthy of an investment multiple times. You also need to consider how far from the source of the loan the asset has traveled. Each person or fund that has a piece of the property will get a piece of the sale, meaning your margin of profit can be slim. And as with any note, you need to make sure the paperwork is in line so you can actually make decisions with the property. When it has passed through many hands to get to you, there is an increased chance that this is not the case.

2. *Purchasing from a credit union or bank*: Banks are willing to offload non-performing loans to save themselves time and money. That is why you can get them for a good price directly from the lender. To make money from this strategy, you need to identify the lender that has the type of notes you want to purchase. Contact the person who controls these loans and makes the decision to sell and be available when they are ready to put them on the market. This relationship is how you will make your money, so take the time to create a strong partnership and you will see the return.

It is not all about the person you purchase from that determines your return; it is about how much you pay for it. Your investment cannot be recouped if you overpay for any asset, including notes. The preferred method for returning your investment is to get your borrower to begin paying once more. If you decide to foreclose the property, keep in mind that before you can receive any profits, if you own the note as a HELOC asset, or Home Equity Line of Credit property, all the back taxes and first and second mortgages must be paid off first. HELOC is a lien from a lender that allows the borrower to receive the most financing, which must be repaid over a predetermined length of time, or a term. The collateral on the note is the house equity the borrower possesses, like a second mortgage.

Working With An Asset Manager or Loan Servicer

The bottom line is that you are the one person that cares the most about your investments and money. No one will care more than you. Despite this fact, seeking professional help with your non-performing and even re-performing liens, can take stress off your shoulders and give you back precious time to use in other areas of your business. Two resources that you can use include asset managers and loan servicers.

Asset managers

These people are experts in "fixing" non-performing or "messy" loans. These people are rare and something you should master on your own. This skill is the art of investing in notes. The first role of an asset manager is to create the relationship with the borrower and then work with them until they have made their loan re-performing. This nuance of working with the people who have sometimes "written off" a "charged off" loan can be a trick. The threat of foreclosure may be necessary to get them ready to begin paying.

Loan Servicers

Do not fall into the trap of thinking that a loan servicer is all you need to make a profit on non-performing notes. They do not fix the problems and make you rich. In fact, they do not "fix" anything. Their role is to be the money collector for re-performing loans. The best use of a loan servicer is to work to get the loan to re-perform and then hand it over to them to collect. If the borrower begins to show signs of slipping back into their old habits, you need to step in and help them stay current. You do this by leveraging your relationship with the borrower that you established, in the beginning, using the tips mentioned above.

If you decide to hire someone to help you maintain your investments, make sure to develop a strong relationship with them. Just like you must set the tone of a professional and respectful relationship with your borrower, you need to do the same with an asset manager or loan servicer. The relationship benefits all parties involved and you want them to value that, and you as a professional. If you approach these relationships with this attitude from the beginning, you will surprise many of them and will probably have a profitable, long-term business ally.

Chapter 4: How to Buy Notes, Even as a Small Investor

Even a small investor can buy and make a profit from real estate notes. The process is similar no matter the type of note you are purchasing, but rather in the collateral and the borrower. Unfortunately, there are no real "rules" on how to purchase a note, probably because this realm is for "investors only". There is no standardization regarding regulations, procedures, and practices. Participants are the ones that determine the process.

In the previous chapter, you learned a couple of places from which you purchase notes; hedge funds and credit unions or banks. For the purpose of this chapter, it is assumed you will be buying notes from a credit union or bank.

After you decide where you are going to look for notes, you need to review the tape and do your due diligence. Due diligence is different depending on your strategy. For example, what you are looking for when considering a note you want to foreclose on, is different than what information you are looking for regarding a non-performing second lien.

The information that is on the tape covers all the relevant collateral and borrower information you need. It is essentially a spreadsheet with numbers related to the note and additional details from the bank about what is being sold.

While reviewing the tape, you need to continually ask yourself what you are willing to invest in the note. When you come up with a range of numbers, chances are you will have several more questions arise.

One of the most often asked questions is, "How much should I pay for a note?" This question cannot be answered with a number, only with more questions. A way to gauge and understand these questions

is to use the loan acquisition suitability and evaluation rating, or
LASER. This is the FDIC's method for understanding a note's value.
You will ask a series of questions and use the rating numbers to
determine if you will purchase the lien.

The questions you ask yourself and the importance of each question
about the note are determined by the type of note and your strategy,
but each consideration will fall into three primary criteria:
lender/seller, collateral, and loan.

Lender/Seller Considerations

- Seller's history
- Participation
- Price of purchase- estimate and expectation
- Advisor versus expectation
- Lender's price expectation
- Balance
- Loan loss reserves per book

Collateral Considerations

- Taxes on the property
- Assessment of the condition of the property
- Environment
- Broker's opinion of value
- Appraisal's value
- Cap rate
- Occupancy
- Size of the property
- Type of property
- Condition of the property
- Year the property was built
- City and state of the property's location
- Net operating income
- Debt service coverage ratio

<u>Loan Considerations</u>

- Condition of the loan file
- Borrower's FICO score
- Borrower's net worth
- Personal guarantee
- Extra collateral
- Evidence of junior lien
- Date of BK filed
- Evidence of bankruptcy
- Litigations
- Date of foreclosure
- Notice of default
- Date of last payment
- Status of the loan
- Forbearance
- Modifications
- Default rate
- Interest rate
- Date of maturity
- Date of origination
- Loan to value currently
- Loan amount originally
- Interest accrued
- Principal balance left unpaid

<u>Submitting an Offer for Purchase</u>

In an ideal situation you will receive the tape and conduct your due diligence prior to making an offer on the note. Sometimes you will have to make an offer before you can dig in. Other times you will get the tape about the same time you need to make the offer.

Regardless of the situation, your lawyer should always be involved in the process. When you are working with a bank you will almost always find yourself interacting with one of their attorneys. If you do not encounter a lawyer, most likely the attorney has already developed the contract and does not want to negotiate. The bank is not taking chances on the contract for purchase, and neither should you.

<u>Negotiations</u>

The process of negotiating with a bank is not a scary or unusual situation. Credit unions, banks, and lenders exchange these notes every day and they are used to the conversations. The process of negotiating is fairly forthright but sometimes it is not smooth. Typically, where it becomes challenging is when the process is not intact and efficiency is lacking. Also, working with large financial institutions usually means you must wait for a long time to accomplish your goals. Being patient and working through the issues can result in a big reward.

To master the process successfully and effectively purchase bank notes, you need to know the following tips:

1. Decision makers are key. Work directly with them.
2. Those that approve the deals should have a good relationship with you. Foster this by spending time getting to know them and building trust in the relationship.
3. Establish a routine of closing on schedule and performing consistently. This creates confidence in your abilities.
4. The credit union or bank and the person in charge of signing off on the deal need to see how working with you will benefit them. Explain and show how you will make the institution money, and the people success.

<u>What to Offer</u>

Knowledge of the current value of notes and your own preference, combine to determine the correct dollar amount to present for a note. When there is limited competition for a note, such as off-market notes, the opportunity for large discounts and more value are attractive. But before you get sucked into a low price, you need to consider all the added costs and those that are subtracted from the value of the note. Things to consider include:

- Options for different investments
- The condition of the real estate market in the asset's local area
- The real estate collaterals value
- Performance status
- Date of maturity
- D-to-I ratio, or "Debt to Income"
- Value predicted for the future
- Amortizing or balloon loan
- Installment payments remaining
- What type of entity owned the origination of the note, private or institution
- Method of calculating interest
- Rate of interest
- Amount of payments remaining
- Credit score
- Seasoning
- Down payment

The Process of the Offer

When you submit an offer, you can do so in a variety of ways; bidding, LOI, indicative bid, or offer to purchase leading to purchase and sale. If you are bidding, you could engage in a sealed or open bid. Banks commonly offer a bidding process for notes being sold to single investors rather than hedge funds. Regardless of the type of bid, this process ensures all the bidders are treated equally and there is no negotiations allowed. It also controls items such as closing times and other terms. A LOI, or Letter of Intent, explains what your term and contingencies are, including your preferred timeline. This is a conversation starter and does not always guarantee the sale. An indicative bid describes what you offer prior to receiving the tape. Banks often hold the specifics of the note private until there is an indicative bid, which allows you to put in the clause, *"As long as due diligence meets expectation."* The final method of making an offer is another form of an LOI or indicative bid - the offer to purchase leading to purchase and Sale. This form contains a binder and describes the timeframe for due diligence. It also includes information about the purchase and sale agreement, which will be finalized prior to closing.

After submitting the offer, you need to include the binder. This can be referred to by other titles. However, it is an amount of money deposited with the note's owner to indicate your level of commitment to the purchase. If you violate the purchase and sale agreement, you risk your binder, but most of the time you can recall the deposit if the note does not withstand your due diligence. You can expect a binder to be about 10% of the price you pay for the property. It is also important to remember that this is not always requested if the seller is looking to close fast. Most respectable sellers will not request money without placing it in escrow. By placing the binder in escrow, you and the seller can ensure that the transaction will meet both party's expectations and the process is relaxed.

Conducting your due diligence can be short or long, depending on the state of the note. However, the range of time can be as little as one week and as long as one month. This is much shorter than the timeframe for a traditional real estate investment, so make sure you are prepared and ready to do your research as fast as possible to close on your deal. When you are finished with your due diligence, you are ready to move on to closing.

<u>How to Close on your Note</u>

When your offer gets accepted, you are now ready to close and take possession of your new asset. To begin the process of closing, you must finish paying for the note. Most of the time, the seller will ask for a wire of the balance. Before you wire that money, make sure you have the following in hand:

- A copy of the deed of trust or mortgage that is identical to the municipality or county's records.

- The borrower's "note," which is the original promissory note the borrower signed that describes the debt terms and the rights of the two parties. (This is essentially what you are purchasing).
- The new lender assignment document. It can also be included in the note, but it must be clearly stated that you are the new servicer of the loan and include your signature as the buyer as well as the seller's. If this comes as a stand-alone document, it is called "allonge".
- While this is optional and often not available, the file gives you details such as additional documents and communication records between the previous lender and the borrower. It is worth asking for, but it is not a typical part of the transaction.

Once you have all those items in your hand, you can wire the balance and take possession of your new asset!

How to Finance Note Buying

Despite being able to purchase a note for pennies on the dollar, you are still looking at a large amount of cash moving from your bank account to the previous lender in a short amount of time if you are doing it alone. The good news is that you can finance, borrow, or pool money to purchase a note.

Financing and Borrowing

Traditional research for financing is not an easy *Google* search away. Instead of blindly hoping to find help in a search engine, look for financing through companies dedicated to helping buy notes or a private lender who can stake your first purchase. Other lenders, such as asset-based or hard money, can be an attractive option, while others have used lines of credit or other loans to help them. The loans can be bridge or business, depending on your strategy. You can also ask a note seller if they know of anyone who has or could finance a note purchase. Finally, dipping into your IRA or 401K can be another option to self-finance.

Pooling

Raising your own funds to purchase notes can seem attractive, but you must be clear on the SEC regulations regarding pooling funds for note purchases. Before exploring this route, hire an attorney to help you make sure that the set up you choose is legal. Ideas for raising capital include:

- Ask current investors who specialize in debt to assist in your business venture
- Create a crowdfunding page for real estate
- Develop new LLC's or partnerships to pool funds for a purchase
- Form a hedge fund
- Cultivate a personal fund for debt investing

Additional Notes on Purchasing Notes

- Make sure you are always entering a deal with integrity. Do not try to swindle or scam another investor with a bad note. The market for buying notes is small and only filled with knowledgeable investors or those wanting to become a player. It will not take long to be discovered if you are not "playing above board."
- If you want to wholesale, buy a lot from hedges or direct from an originating institution.
- If you are looking for passive income generated from your savings, pick up notes from brokers or hedges to reap the long-term rewards. This means you are not intending to "flip" the note.

Chapter 5: Expected Returns

As explained in the previous chapters, once you figure out how buying and profiting from notes is possible, you can expect to make good returns. But you may now be wondering what kinds of returns you can expect. As with most investments in any sense, this can fluctuate minute-to-minute depending on market conditions, among other things. But overall, if you approach note-buying knowledgeable, you can expect to see a good profit fairly fast. In this chapter, you will learn some important considerations regarding your return, see some examples of returns on an investment, and finally, walk away with a simple guide to use for valuation of a potential investment. This guide is easily replicable in *Excel*, where you can program the cells to do the math for you, giving you a tool to use quickly and easily any time you are looking at a potential note. It is not a guarantee of profit, but it is a good estimator! Plug it in and play around with it. You will find what you are able and comfortable with in no time.

Before you get into finding out your profit potential, you need to know what the structure of payment has been set at. The common mortgage note structures include floating-rate and fixed rate and a combination of a fixed/float. This combination is most common in commercial notes, which will be described in a later chapter. Another common structure is a balloon. A floating-rate refers to a loan's interest rate that changes based on a certain index. It can alter every day or every year, depending on the terms of the note. A fixed-rate never changes during the lifetime of the note. A balloon means that the borrower can have a fixed-rate, but after a predefined period of time, the principal is due. This period is set prior to the end of the loan's term.

Case Study

The due diligence on a potential note purchase had the following details:

Collateral- $287,000 for five duplexes

Loan's principal balance left unpaid- $193,000

Cash flow- Subsidized program resulting in monthly income of $5,000

Borrower- A troubled LLC that was in court for a variety of reasons not associated with the ownership of the duplexes, and did not purchase the real estate considering all the financial expectations of a landlord, such as repair costs and monthly maintenance fees.

The credit union holding the note was seeking to offload it because of the problems with the borrower and the fact that they had stopped paying their mortgage. The reason the borrower had stopped paying was that they were under the impression that they had sold the property. However, it would not close for another 90 days.

The lender was offering the note for these properties at $100,000 but it was negotiated to $80,000. The reason the credit union agreed was that it could be closed in less than one day. This was attractive because this smaller lender needed the "bad" loan off their books as soon as possible and this was an easy solution for them.

Once the assets note was in the possession of the new lender, the foreclosure process began. Basically, the borrower was given a demand letter. When no money was received, a default notice was given, and the courthouse processed the notice. Three months after the notice was issued the property was supposed to be foreclosed at the courthouse. Through the process, a capable attorney was present to manage the documentation. The cost of this process was about $3,000.

When the new lender went to the courthouse for the foreclosure, instead, they received a payoff check. The sale that was set in motion prior to purchasing the note finalized about two hours before the foreclosure was complete.

The payoff check was for $193,000. The original investment was $80,000, plus the $3,000 invested in the foreclosure process. The new lender made approximately $110,000 in three months. As expected, there were other fees to be paid out for the transaction, but overall, the profit was impressive for the little time the asset was in the new lender's possession without them needing to do anything to the real estate.

Alternative Scenarios to the Case Study

In the above example, the new lender was an investor looking to make an immediate profit. Instead of foreclosing on the property, you could consider alternative solutions like working it out with the borrower to get their note re-performing. Once the note gets back to performance, it is more valuable to resell. This is "flipping" the note. For example, in the above scenario, if you get the borrower to become current on their payments, you could potentially resell the loan for $160,000, essentially doubling your initial investment in a short amount of time.

Another option is to get the loan re-performing, gathering the payments each month for the loan from the borrower, plus principal, to enjoy the passive income and pay off your investment over time instead of immediately. This is a long-term strategy.

A final alternative, which is the "ideal" scenario in the case study, is to foreclose on the property allowing you to collect market value rent for each duplex, which was valued at $1,500 per unit, or $3,000 for each duplex, monthly. This would gross $180,000 each year for an asset that you only invested $83,000 in. If you did not want to collect rent on the property after you foreclose, you could place the duplexes on the market and sell them for market value, which was appraised at $287,000. This alternative would potentially be the most profitable strategy resulting in a profit of $204,000, not including the fees for selling and time for the process to complete.

This case study and the alternative solutions is one example of how you can make a profit buying notes through different scenarios, but also how outside forces can change your strategy in the blink of an eye. It is important that you consider all potential scenarios before you make an offer so that no matter what happens, you walk away in the black.

Return Math and Guide

The math used in calculating your return is actually rather simple. To illustrate the process, imagine you find a lender wanting to offload a $20,000 note at 20% for twenty years. The payment for the mortgage is $264.30. When you do your due diligence, you decide that the collateral and borrower are in order and submit an offer with the goal of a 15% return on your cash investment.

When you make an offer to purchase the note, you determine the amount you need to discount the note to create the return of 15%. In this scenario, that amount is $16,382.16. Assuming the lender holding the note accepts this original offer, you can enjoy a much larger rate of return than the average 8% in the hard asset market in real estate. This large rate is the reason to invest in notes.

Create a calculator to determine the return for yourself. The basic information required includes:

- Monthly payments required for a twenty-year mortgage, which is 240- N
- Interest rate percentage, in this scenario it is 20%- I
- Current note value, which is $20,000- PV
- Monthly payment based on the preceding information, which is calculated at $264.30- PMT

To create your own calculator, place yourself in a position to make wise decisions quickly on a potential note. It's a game of paper, which you can master by increasing your return rate and strategizing with other players to both your and their advantage.

Use different return percentages to find out what you should offer and how much you can make over time. This way if negotiating is below what you are willing to accept, and you know when to walk away.

Below is a table that can provide guidance to you when figuring out if the investment is worth your time and money. Again, this is a tool to help you, not a definitive resource that guarantees your financial success. Use this to help you but do not rely solely on this information. You must also use your knowledge, intuition, and experience to determine if a certain note is worth pursuing.

Make sure to change the red terms to create a more interactive analysis of NPV:

Prog. Considerations		
Present Freddie Mac Rate	4.6%	
Floor of the Present Interest Rate	2.0%	
Present Status & Info. Of Origination of Loan		
Starting Amount for Loan	$250,000	Information for Loan and Borrower

Starting Term for Amortization	360	
Starting Interest Rate	6.000%	
Yes or No- Is this an Interest Only Loan	YES	
Present Unpaid Principal Balance	$150,000	
Present Interest Rate	6.000%	
Outstanding Term	310	
Length of Past Due (In Months)	4	
State of the Asset	ID	
Escrow or Advances	$256	
Present Payment to Mortgage Monthly	$1,250.00	Adjust as needed; terms of starting loan are used to find the payments for IO and P&I
Present Payment on Interest	$1,250.00	
Present Payment on Principal	$0.00	
Interest Past Due	$3,750	
Escrow and Accrued Interest Factored into Adjusted Unpaid	$154,006	

Principal Balance		
Status of Borrower		
Income Monthly *	$4,000	
Insurance and Taxes Monthly	$150	
Foreclosure Set-up		
Escrow and Accrued Interest Factored into Adjusted Unpaid Principal Balance	$154,006	
Value at Present	$190,000	
Prediction of Appreciation for Price of Home	-3%	Adjust as required for Individual Asset
Discount of REO Stigma	10%	
Sale of Foreclosure (Months)	2	
Sale of REO (Months)	4	
Cost Disposition of REO & Foreclosure	$5,740	
Advance Escrow/ Predicted Interest	$2,400	

Value of REO	$157,730	
Loss of PV at 0 Cure	$3,639	
Rate of Cure	12%	Adjust as required for borrower and loan information
WTD Loss and the Likelihood of PV	$3,203	

Current Modification of PV		
Reasonable Level of DTI	30%	
Adjusted Payment	$1,090	
30 Yr. Term Interest Rate	3.0%	**Outstanding term for amortization used for adjustment**
40 Yr. Term Interest Rate	3.3%	
Adjusted Payment Successful Because of Necessary Adjusted Terms of the Loan		
Escrow and Accrued Interest Factored into Adjusted Unpaid Principal Balance	$154,006	Same as foreclosure set-up adjusted UPB

		Choose the max necessary to a 30 or 40 yr. term or floor of the prog.
Adjusted Interest Rate	2.98%	
Adjusted Payment	$1,090	
Adjusted Term of Loan	310	
Adjusted Complete Amortization Payment	$712.65	These factors are necessary to factor the total of forbearance of principal
Variance between Reasonable Payment	$0.00	
Forbearance of Principal	$0.00	
Cash Flow Lowered by PV	($11,204.14)	
Re-default Prior to Adjustment Value Assumption		
Interest Rate Prior to Re-default	35%	
Length to Re-default (in Months)	2	Adjust as required for loan and borrower information and location of the property
Present Date Prediction of Appreciation to the Price of the Asset	-3%	
Advance Escrow/	$5,304	

Predicted Interest		
Value of REO	$154,826	
Projected Cost of PV	$1,437	
Adjusted Value		
Adjusted Value	($6,663)	
Adjustment Advantage	($9,865.40)	
Pass or Fail- What is the result of the NPV Test	FAIL	Short Sale should be considered
Terms Related to the Adjustment		
Starting Payment Difference (%)	-12.8%	
Anticipated Borrower's Monthly Payments:		
1st Month	$712.65	
60th Month	$781.23	9.6%
72nd Month	$823.93	5.5%
84th Month	$823.93	0.0%
96th Month	$823.93	0.0%
108th Month	$823.93	0.0%

Chapter 6: Common Challenges of Note Investing

It is not wise to invest in something, especially something as large as a mortgage note, without first considering all the challenges and potential negative consequences of the choice. As with anything, there are disadvantages to think about, especially the risks associated with them. The more you invest and get experience, the less the risks will deter you. In fact, your questions and concerns may morph over time. Despite your experience, there will always be something to learn and common challenges you will face.

Policies and Compliance

Compliance challenges have become a major challenge in recent years. This is partially thanks to the development of the Consumer Financial Protection Bureau, or the CFPB, and the start of Dodd-Frank. The federal government has become more involved in lending-companies and with other note-holders as well. States have also become more involved with requirements for licensing but each state continues to be different. There is a lack of constant state regulations. This means there is a web of policies you need to navigate through. This is even more complicated when working in multiple states.

Even when you are small and just starting to invest in notes, you need to be knowledgeable of compliance issues. This covers topics ranging from working with third party vendors to Fair Debt Collection Practices Act, or FDCPA. Even getting access to information about the borrower can be a breach of compliance.

Legal Considerations

When you purchase a note, one of the largest expenses you will incur is related to your legal needs. This is one of the largest "disadvantages" of buying notes. The legal process starts when you need to foreclose on a property and have explored all the options to work out with the borrower. The need to foreclose on the asset sets in motion timelines, expenses, and requirements that are different from one state to the next.

Part of the legal considerations includes understanding your state in terms of if you are dealing in a "judicial" or "deed of trust" state. This information will give you a clue at the start on how long you can expect to spend in the foreclosure process. It also will determine how you hire legal representation for the foreclosure process, delivering the letter demanding payment, submitting a completed "lis pendens", entering your offer to buy, and setting the timeline to eject the borrower from the asset.

Other than the above-mentioned legal challenges, you need to also consider if the borrower files bankruptcy. This opens another door for delayed timelines and legal binds. Things like back payments on homeowner's associations, liens from the municipality, and back taxes are other legal issues you may face when buying notes. Occasionally, you do need to go to the property and make changes to it, such as switch out the locks, change codes, and paint to bring it up to expectation in the neighborhood.

Problems with Collateral

Documents outlining your asset's collateral can sometimes be in disarray; you could be missing important documents. Sometimes it can even lack a copy of the starting note or the note's assignment. Even the allonge could be missing. Beyond the paperwork, you could also have issues with the actual collateral. It has happened where the asset was once in acceptable condition but has dropped in upkeep over time. The city may have also torn down or condemned the site.

Conditions of the Market

The mortgage note is backed up by an actual piece of real estate. This means any threat to the actual property is a threat to your note's value. One of these threats is the decline of the property's fair market value. If the value drops below your investment, you risk having to foreclose and not cover the entire amount of the loan you are responsible for.

Large Capital Investment

If you are investing in secondary liens, you must consider the state of the primary lien. If the primary forecloses prior to you, your note will be erased, and you will be left with no asset from your investment. To protect yourself you can either start the process quickly to foreclose or bid to purchase the senior lien to make sure your position is secure, no matter what happens.

Benefits from Taxes are Limited

A traditional investment in real estate comes with the tax benefit of appreciation and depreciation. This is not the case with a mortgage note even though the original investment can be just as large. It is possible to get a break on your taxes if you use your retirement account, such as an IRA, to invest in the note. Another opportunity for a tax break is if you create a non-profit note business to buy and sell the assets.

Appreciation is Lacking

The actual property enjoys the benefit of appreciation. The only way for you to receive any "appreciation" is if you receive an advance from a corporation on the starting unpaid principal balance, or UPB, you charge a late fee for a missed payment, or there are missed payments you need to collect. At times, there is something called "phantom appreciation" for a note. This occurs when you buy a discounted note that is only partially covered by equity. If the property's value improves because the overall market increases, the mortgage and property value goes up. This is not something that happens often but is a nice increase to your return when it does.

Investor/Note Holder Hold-Up's

Sometimes the disadvantages you face are not external problems, but rather internal challenges you need to overcome. These can be as simple as changing your internal dialogue of your success and motives, to taking strategic actions to improve borrower relations. Some of the challenges most new note investors face are:

1. _They accept "No" as "No."_ New investors can become discouraged when their bids are denied. It is important that you do not give in easily. Be flexible and prepared to approach the investment in different ways. This also means that if you get stuck with an unsecured lien because the primary lien is foreclosed, you do not need to walk away from the deal. Instead you can search for a way to recuperate your investment. Exploring other avenues like working with the borrower not the property for repayment, offload to an attorney specializing in collections, or find a platform for exchange you can sell the property on.

2. _They get stuck in the quicksand._ Actually, taking action can be daunting, but it is important that you make the results happen. Novice investors react to situations when confident, and experienced investors anticipate challenges and mediate them before they become a major problem. Do not wait for the borrower to get in contact with you. You need to have a strategy in place to call, mail, and email the borrower until you speak with them. Even having a loan servicer or attorney ready to step in to help get in touch can be a wise, proactive strategy.

3. _Nothing is ever their fault; someone else is responsible for a "bad" deal._ You are human. You will make a mistake or a bad call. Do not blame the borrower, or previous note holder or market conditions for what happened. Be accountable for yourself and accept responsibility for

your choices. The important thing is what you learn from the mistake, so you do not make them again in the future. Also, it is important that you observe other note investors to learn from their mistakes so you can avoid those as well. For example, when you are starting out, you are not experienced reviewing the tape and conducting your due diligence. This results in loopholes, such as never receiving the starting note or your assignment. If this happens, you run the risk of not being able to record your assignment and begin the process of foreclosing if necessary. This gives the primary lien the opportunity to foreclose before you get the documentation in line, clearing out your lien and leaving you in the red. Accepting your role in this result means you can learn how to avoid this in your future purchases. You can submit an indicative bid to make sure that documentation as important as this is clean before purchasing.

4. *You do not have a system.* There are several documents you need to have access to at all times for your notes. These are what allow you to take action as needed on your asset to make sure you get your return. If you do not have an organized system, you risk losing important information and not being able to access it when you need to. You need to maintain good logs and files on your notes. This even includes the measurable outcomes, your due diligence completed, and data that was reviewed.

5. *You avoid creativity in favor of comfort.* If you are afraid of thinking outside of the "not purchasing" box, you risk not being able to reap the big returns. Non-performing liens that you want to rework require creativity, just like any business. The best way to work out a lien that is not performing requires that you talk with your borrower to find a "win/win" situation. This is different for each borrower.

6. *You are a lone wolf.* This business is not good for you if you think you can do it alone or want to be in it all by yourself. This is a business of relationships and you need to network to develop a strong professional base. These are the people you will turn to when

you need assistance. You want to have at least one mentor to be able to call at any time to help you along your journey to purchasing notes. Even after you are an experienced note buyer, do not forget the value of a coach to help your business grow and scale up.

7. *They do not take the time to understand the math.* This is beyond just understanding the formulas and math to calculate a return-worth investment. You also need to understand the numbers related to the industry, such as Freddie Mac rates and UPC. Having this understanding also creates confidence in yourself and others.

8. *They alienate those around them.* Vendors and borrowers are people. You need to work with them constantly when working with notes. If you alienate them and do not build a relationship with them, they are less likely to be open with you about disadvantages they identify, or to help find a resolution to a problem. This means you either need to work on your people skills or find a person who will mediate the relationships so the rapport is positively established. This one trait is quite possibly the most important trait to your success or failure.

These eight traits can make or break you as an investor in notes. These characteristics are somewhat similar to investing in a hard real estate. The major difference in your skillset is collections, particularly for notes that are not performing. Thankfully, learning how to embody the positive habits and overcome the negative are not insurmountable, just distinctive.

Despite all the above-mentioned threats and challenges of investing in notes, there are methods of overcoming the disadvantages that make it worth it. Of course, this chapter only covers some of the major concerns and there will be unique scenarios that are not mentioned, but in general, the potential for returns is worth it. The investors that thrive in this industry work around the risks just like hard real estate investors work around those innate challenges.

When you encounter a problem when investing in notes, you can hire help to navigate the tangle of regulations or compliance standards. You can also use other money other than your own to invest, lowering your risk of losing all your savings and safety-net in a bad deal. Loan servicers, asset managers, and attorneys are all your allies in making sure your investment is fruitful. Learning how and perfecting your due diligence methods will also make sure you can be confident in the Fair Market Value, or FMV, the condition of the property, occupants of the asset, and valid liens. In addition, you can scale this investment easily, allowing you to gain experience fast, thus increasing your returns and lowering the novice mistakes swiftly. This can more than compensate for the challenges you will face.

Chapter 7: Commercial Note Investing

Investing in commercial real estate, whether it is a physical property or in notes, requires a different knowledge and approach. It can be more challenging but the market is large. Despite the daunting position, it can actually be fairly easy to enter and succeed; you just need to know what you are getting into. Commercial notes are loans provided to businesses and not individuals. These loans are mortgage notes and commercial and industrial-backed loans. If a business is over three months late on their payments, their loan is considered non-performing. This is the most common reason a loan is classified as non-performing, but there are other reasons as well that will be explained later.

Varieties of Commercial Notes that are Non-performing

There are different types of loans for commercial purposes and you must be familiar with them before you consider purchasing your first commercial note. This is because your approach will be different for each kind. It is definitely not a "one-size-fits-all" strategy. The two major types of commercial loans are mortgage notes and non-mortgage notes. A mortgage note is secured by physical real estate while non-mortgage notes are not.

Mortgage Notes

Loans that are given to multi-family situations are considered a common commercial mortgage loan. Buildings that are mixed-use or have more than five dwellings in them are considered multi-family mortgages. If there is a mixed-use building with five or more units, and at least one is used for residential purposes, the note is classified as multi-family. Another example of a commercial mortgage note is a construction note. When a company is building one to four single-family houses, the loans acquired to complete the construction are attached to the property. These loans include the actual construction of the house, the land, and other development needs. A third commercial mortgage note example is a property loan. There are two main types of commercial property loans: Non-owner and owner-occupied.

Non-owner Occupied Commercial Property

This is a property that is intended as an investment only. This includes buildings like land intended for developing, mixed-use structures, strip plazas, shopping malls, and office buildings.

Owner Occupied Commercial Property

If a business owner receives a loan to run a business out of a property, this is considered "owner-occupied." The property can be partially or fully used for their business. These include mixed-use structures, industrial sites and warehouses, gas stations, restaurants, shopping stores, churches, medical complexes, and smaller buildings with offices.

Non-mortgage Notes

There are two forms of debt for non-mortgage commercial notes: C and I, or Commercial and Industrial debt, and unsecured debt. C and I are the most common loan for a non-mortgage note. A loan could be backed by assets, inventory, or equipment that is financed instead of by property. The business owners, cosigners, and borrowers sign a personal guarantee for the assets securing on the debt. Unsecured notes involve lines of credit, advances from merchants, and credit cards for businesses.

Just like residential note buying, commercial notes can be bought as performing or non-performing and the price will reflect the work necessary to reap your return. As a commercial note investor, you can expect various advantages and risks with either.

Non-performing Commercial Notes

Purchasing a commercial loan that is no longer performing provides you as the investor a host of challenges and opportunities. Typically the notes are non-performing because the borrower has not kept up on their payments. However, there are other reasons it does not perform. These can be the fact that the collateral changed in value, if the business borrowed against the principal in a poor action, the property was transferred to another business, paperwork for the insurance was lost, taxes on the property are behind, or the loan has not been refinanced since the balloon matured.

Commercial note strategies for non-performing liens usually fall into two categories: workout the loan with the borrower to bring in monthly cash flow or take over the asset from the borrower to force them to make payments again.

<u>The benefits of purchasing a Commercial Loan that is not performing:</u>

1. Sellers of commercial notes typically provide steep discounts to investors in addition to exit strategies that are vaster than on residential notes.
2. Commercial borrowers are usually motivated to help you find the largest foreclosure price and are required to show their books and open the property for bidders to see.
3. A commercial note is usually more expensive with a larger return potential, but the time frame is similar to a residential note. Investing in commercial notes means you can do more in the same amount of time.
4. Commercial borrowers normally enter into an agreement with all the information and ability. Courts assume they are capable business people and therefore settle on the side of the lender, making the process of fixing defaults much faster.
5. A borrower whose note is non-performing is usually sophisticated and well off. This means that if you lose money in the foreclosure process, you can continue looking for the remainder from the borrower.

<u>The challenges of purchasing a Commercial Loan that is not performing:</u>

1. Changes in the market and rapidly moving prices during lengthy work-outs, the process of bankruptcy, or negotiations with borrowers that are aggressive, can result in you not being able to recover your investment.
2. Bankruptcy costs a lot of money and is a lengthy process in the commercial setting. Most often the investor walks away with at least their investment, except when there are major changes to the market value of the property.
3. If you end up taking over a "dirty" property, you risk being held liable for its condition. There can be a host of environmental problems with a property that may not be evident during your due diligence process or the foreclosure process.

Performing Commercial Notes

The most attractive reason you should consider looking into a performing note is that the return is protected and stable. You have constant cash flow because the note is consistently paying and secured with a tangible asset. If you are nervous about the risks involved in purchasing notes this strategy can be attractive.

<u>The benefits of purchasing a Commercial Loan that is performing:</u>

1. The burden of managing the note is lower.
2. A hard asset backs the investment.
3. Cash flow is stable and consistent.
4. You gather a higher return on the principal payments of a commercial loan that is paying on time.
5. You can seek compensation from the borrower if they fail to pay, or the balance of the foreclosure does not cover your investment.

<u>The challenges of purchasing a Commercial Loan that is performing:</u>

1. Asset managers and time managing the note can cut into the return on a commercial investment quickly.
2. Borrowers that are currently paying can slip and your cash flow can turn into a challenge because it is now non-performing.
3. Initial value estimations of the collateral and note can be incorrect.

Places to Look for Commercial Notes to Purchase

As with residential note investing, the process starts with locating a note that is for sale. This particular task is challenging and coveted. To find these notes, there are three places you can research: services, credit unions or banks, and from owners directly.

Direct from Owner

Financing by the owner when an investor sells is a fairly common strategy you will encounter. Properties with low balances are especially prone to this market. When an investor sells the property, they are able to reduce the implications on their taxes. Instead of dealing with the tax liability immediately, the investor can "hold the paper" and spread the liability over several years. Search for terms such as "seller finance," "owner carry," or "seller will carry" in real estate listings. These terms indicate that the seller probably has additional notes.

Check sites like For Sale by Owner websites or *Craigslist*. In addition, you should create *Google* alerts and IFTTT so you are notified when commercial loans are listed online.

Credit Unions or Banks

This is considered the main locations for finding commercial notes for sale. Almost 1/3 of the lending institutions like credit unions and banks carry commercial loans and real estate. This is why you can go to them to find both performing and non-performing loans they want to get rid of for a large discount. To make the time looking worthwhile, you need to learn which banks have a selection of commercial loans and if they are willing to sell them. Once you identify the right place, you need to develop and foster the relationship with the decision maker. After you have a strong rapport, you need to submit offers that are acceptable for the asset they want to offload.

Servicers

This unique role refers to an organization that is designed to work on notes that are either sub-performing or non-performing. The role of this organization or the individual servicer is to change the note to re-perform or help you sell the lien. Another form of service refers to auction sites and broker's specializing in commercial notes to help you sell and also find new investments for the future.

Many investors are worried about purchasing commercial notes, primarily because they view the process as complex or too complicated. In reality, commercial notes are almost identical to residential. There are only a couple of exclusions. One of the biggest differences is the borrower. They tend to be more cooperative than residential borrowers. In addition, these borrowers are more knowledgeable. If you need or want to foreclose on the property, most of the time the borrower will understand and know the process and the process will be smoother.

Also, in a commercial setting, the legal side is on the side of the note holder. The borrower is not as favored in the laws compared to you as the note holder or lender. Finally, the numbers are just higher. For example, you can see up to a 20% return on a note for about the same amount of time for a residential or commercial loan. This means you have to decide if you would want to receive that 20% return on a residential note that is valued at $200,000 or a commercial note that is valued at $2,000,000 with the same time investment. You reap almost twenty times more profit with a commercial note for doing about the equivalent quantity of effort.

A Side Note: You Need to Research

When you purchase in a commercial note, you must research and understand the market. The residential market is easily understood by looking around at what is visible online. A deeper dive is required to see and understand the market for commercial notes.

Another consideration that requires your research is related to collateral. You must take the time to untangle complicated collateral. And commercial borrowers are more knowledgeable than those of a residential note. Collateral can be affected by factors such as zoning, permits, and environment.

Of course, there are other considerations and research you need to do before investing a large amount of cash required to secure a commercial note. This chapter is to give you the overview of the opportunity and potential risk so you realize it can be worth your time if you do it smart.

Flipping a Loan Case Study

A gas station that was not performing note became available and a commercial note investor that enjoyed purchasing non-performing liens credit unions became interested. This investor not only bought notes, but created them as well, but only for commercial borrowers. When this investor purchases the gas station's note, it came from a little credit union. The lender only had the one location, which is very tiny for a lender. This small credit union had purchased the gas station's note from another lender in hopes of making money. When they realized they had paid too much for the asset and were not making money, they decided instead to foreclose and sell it to a private investor.

The gas station had a balance of approximately $1.9 million and the credit union agreed to sell the note for $850,000. The investor submitted an offer to buy only because they understood the market. This incredible discount allowed the investor to take over the foreclosure process and bring the asset to bidding. The borrower cooperated with the process and allowed bidders to view the property. When the bidding began, the bidders almost all had been vetted prior to the sale or was able to sell the asset at auction for $1.5 million. The entire process took approximately two months. The investor walked away from the proceedings with a return of $650,000.

Conclusion

Thank you for making it through to the end of *Real Estate Note Investing: How Buying Distressed and Profitable Mortgages Can Skyrocket Your Investment Income*, let's hope it was informative and able to provide you with all of the tools you need to achieve your goals whatever they may be.

The next step is to decide if you want and are able to start with residential note investing or commercial. Weigh the pros and cons of each strategy and pick a route you want to take. Once you decide, then narrow down the kind of note you plan to go after. Of course, you can be fluid and change your strategies as an opportunity arises. However, now is the time to determine what you would prefer to work with; performing or non-performing. After that, the fun can really begin! It is time to find your first note!

Dive in, work a strategy maybe using the calculator provided in this book, and get ready to see your reward. Hopefully, the information in this book was instructive and informative. Ideally, the concepts you learned here can be easily applied to your professional goals; knowing you are taking a risk that can offer you high returns for your investment savvy. Now is the time to take these tools you have received here and use them in the real world to make yourself some real money!

<u>NOTES</u>

Printed in the USA
CPSIA information can be obtained
at www.ICGtesting.com
CBHW070932190424
7136CB00043B/1600